FINDING Love in the MIDST of PAIN

Dr. Gwendolyn D. Boyd-Shields

Finding Love in the Midst of Pain

Copyright © 2024 by Dr. Gwendolyn D. Boyd-Shields. All rights reserved.

No part of this publication may be reproduced, stored in a retrieval system or transmitted in any way by any means, electronic, mechanical, photocopy, recording or otherwise without the prior permission of the author except as provided by USA copyright law.

The opinions expressed by the author are not necessarily those of URLink Print and Media.

1603 Capitol Ave., Suite 310 Cheyenne, Wyoming USA 82001
1-888-980-6523 | admin@urlinkpublishing.com

URLink Print and Media is committed to excellence in the publishing industry.

Book design copyright © 2024 by URLink Print and Media. All rights reserved.

Published in the United States of America
Library of Congress Control Number: 2024924801
ISBN 978-1-68486-992-3 (Paperback)
ISBN 978-1-68486-996-1 (Digital)

14.10.24

PREFACE

This book is written to encourage those who have never found or lost love. You see I lost love, but it came back to me in a form that will forever stay in my heart. Yes, in my heart is where truly love came for me. On our journey of romance, heartache, and heartbreak, we find a treasure. That treasure is none other than Jesus Christ of Nazareth. I found him to be the one thing that will never fail or disappoint me. I, however, have disappointed Him on more than one occasion, but He never held it against me. I am truly thankful for His love, encouragement, wisdom, friendship, and most of all His peace. His peace has inspired me to write this book. Through His peace, I have found joy, happiness, sorrow, pain, laughter, contentment, excitement, tears, and all the emotions a person can express. I hope those of you who read this book can find a way to express the hidden emotions that you keep locked away. I use to hide my emotions, but through love I was able to unleash my fears, joy, happiness, sorrow, and even tears. Tears were the hardest things for me to unleash. I found it difficult to cry even when I hurt the most. Through the love of Jesus Christ of Nazareth, I was able to release the tears and let them freely flow. It is a joy to know and feel the love of Jesus Christ of Nazareth. I charge you, to let your emotions run freely and escape into the world of peace and joy that only the Son of God can give.

May the blessings of God smile forever upon
your existence now and forevermore!

Gwendolyn D. L. Boyd
Minister of the Gospel of Peace

Contents

Chapter 1 Introduction 11

Chapter 2 How Is Love Defined 15

Chapter 3 Who Are The Best People To Love 21

Chapter 4 I Hurt How Can I Love Someone 27

Chapter 5 I'm Not Whole How Can I Love 35

Chapter 6 I Want To Love 43

Chapter 7 I Found Him 49

Chapter 1

Introduction

What is love? Why is love so important to human beings? Why do humans desire love? Can love truly be expressed? Is it an imaginary thing? Is it splendid? How do I hold on to it forever? These are the many questions that we or someone we know ask. Is there an easy definition to love? Of course, there is not. We search our hearts, our minds, books, our Bible, and any other sources imaginable to find the answer. We even look to others to help define love for us. There is only one true way to find love, and that is through the knowledge of knowing Jesus Christ of Nazareth. Why is it found only through Him? That is a question that I shall hope to answer in the following chapters of this book.

> *"I pray that you find that real, mature, and lasting love that shall stand and endure all the tests of time."*

Get a cup of tea, a glass of water, or your favorite brew of coffee, and join me as I journey through the world of love. For it is a journey, I have traveled more than once. I must say I was grateful to have taken the trips. The greatest thing about love was finding it a second time. I found that a more mature love is far better than an immature, infatuation. Finding that special person to love is hard, but it can be achieved. The lesson that I learned during the loving process is that loving someone is easy. The hard part comes from getting love back in return.

Sometimes, what we send out doesn't come back to us the exact way we have sent it, but we must wait for the love that God wants us to have. We can invest in the wrong people, places, and things, but only when we let Jesus Christ of Nazareth be our focus and center are we complete and loved. Through this journey, I hope that you find that completeness that gravitates throughout everything that you say and do. Let your love be that which attracts others to you now and throughout all eternity. That is why it is so important **"Finding Love in The Midst of Pain"**.

It is great to love, but far greater to be loved!!!

Chapter 2

How Is Love Defined

When you think of love, what runs through your mind? Is it a bright, joyful feeling that is invigorating, or is it a conscience decision just to be kind or do as well as say extremely nice things? I like to think of love as a joyful experience that consumes. I like the expressiveness and impulsiveness that is displayed toward others. When I am in love, the world seems more beautiful, more alive, more colorful, sunnier, greener, and just more fun. I truly enjoy being in love. I feel as if nothing could go wrong, and that nothing will. Even on sad occasions, I still feel a sense of wonderfulness. There is a spring in my steps, a song in my heart, and a huge smile on my face. On those days, I need very little makeup. People around me say that I am glowing. It is not just an outward thing, but something internal. The words I use to express myself are also colorful, vibrant, and full of energy. When I look at the Bible, the Word of God, I find myself drawn to the Song of Solomon. I truly like the verse that says, **"Many waters cannot quench love, nor can the floods drown it"** (8:7). That signifies my emotions to the depths of my heart. With love, I do believe your heart is the driving force behind your actions. I do not believe you can love without bringing your heart along. The heart is the central area of standards in that we live. Our heart dictates how we do things, and what our actions will look like. The Bible says in Matthew 12:35, "A good man out of the good treasure of the heart bringeth forth good things: and an evil man out of the evil treasure bringeth forth evil things". Our heart dictates our actions. Jesus went even further and states in verse 34, "For out of the abundance of the heart the mouth speaketh". Just imagine this, "You speak what is in your heart". We should have a "love language", but do we? What type of language are we promoting?

Expressions are usually governed by the heart. The exception to this would be your thoughts. The Bible says, "So as a man thinkest so is he". So, if you think you are in love, then maybe you may express it as if it were the real thing. People are looking for sincere genuine love. I know that was what I was looking for and still am. Realness makes things better. As Cheryl Lynn said, "Got To Be Real".

"True love must be expressed."

The real thing comes in many forms. A heartfelt smile, heartfelt hug, money, a heartfelt kiss, a greeting card, jewelry, perfume, books, clothing, a specially made blanket, a pleasant phone call, a visit to your workplace or home, a fabulous date, encouraging words, and the list can go on and on.

In the Bible, love is expressed in many ways such as healing, a welcome to someone's home, a meal, or even a place of refuge from your enemies. I personally like the scriptures coming from I Corinthians chapter 13. They say, "Love suffers long, and is kind;

envieth not; vaunteth not itself, is not puffed up, doth not behave itself unseemingly, seeketh not her own, is not easily provoked, thinketh no evil; rejoiceth not in iniquity, but rejoiceth in the truth, beareth all things, believeth all things, hopeth all things, endureth all things". How more real can you get than this? Can you truly achieve this kind of love, and can you give this kind of love? That is the question to ask yourself. Giving is the fundamental foundation of love. In order to receive love, you must first be willing to give. Giving teaches us how to promote the other individual. Some people are natural givers, and others are natural takers. How do they balance each other? It is through love. I believe the person who takes learns from the giver to give while the giver learns from the taker to receive. This is how balance is created. The old saying is "opposites attract". It surely works in science why not in love? If you are a taker, learn to give sometimes, and feel the joy it brings to the ones you love. If you are a giver, learn to receive sometimes from those who want to share their love with you. It may be hard at first to adjust to a new way of doing things, but eventually, you will wonder why it took so long to get to this stage of your life. **It is truly great to be loved and feel loved!!!**

    Time makes adjustments to our realities. It is through time we learn to change our hearts and mindset. Our hearts are the biggest area of adjustment we will encounter in our lifetime. Changing your heart will be the greatest challenge you will ever face. When someone breaks your heart after you have placed it into their hands to hold, can be devastating. Learning to trust again can be difficult as well as complicated. It is not like riding a bike or a gentle horse. From these experiences, we can get on again without much thought or consideration. A broken heart requires time to heal, forgive, and sometimes forget, if possible! All of this requires time. For some, the timing may be a lifetime, for others, it may only be until they meet the next kind and generous person. Love will take place and life will have joy and gladness. Life will have a freshness of spring and an odor of expensive perfume. It will be as lovely as a flower and as gentle as a newborn baby.

Would you not like to experience this phenomenon in your lifetime? Would you not like to feel this euphoria of passion? Would you not like to be and feel loved? Take a chance and open your heart. Feel! Feel! Feel! You will be glad that you allowed yourself to have your heart open to someone special. For, that person will always be special to you no matter how long they stay in your life. They will always be special to you, and you will love them throughout the years. The sound of their name will bring a smile to your face. Their face will bring a song of joy and love to your lips. Their body will be a sense of strength and passion to your eyes. In other words, love awakens your senses. It is like the sweet smell of fragrant flowers no matter where you are or what you are doing. Just thinking of them shall arouse you in ways you would have never imagined. Surely, **it is good to be loved and feel loved!!!**

Chapter 3

Who Are The Best People To Love

Loving can be a complex thing to be done or displayed. Loving someone can be one-sided as well. Just because you love someone doesn't mean that they will reciprocate. How do you determine if someone is worthy of your love or the love you have to give? You don't! This is a situation where Jesus plays a major role. It is Jesus that makes this judgment. We, however, must be willing to follow in His desires. We are the ones who sometimes feel as if we can not love certain individuals. This judgment may be based on skin color, height, weight, social status, economics, religious background, geographical location, gender, and I just don't like them. How many times have you suggested to a friend about considering someone of the opposite sex and their response is "I just don't like them"!

They could be well groomed, great personality, good job, all-around nice person, but you get that response, "I just don't like them". What makes a person likeable enough to be loved? What makes them likeable enough to be marriage material? What makes them likeable enough for you to consider them as a marriage partner? We as individuals have the strangest answers, but yet, sometimes we want the same things. Go figure! When we look at the Bible, God loves us without constraint or the hang-ups we have with one another. God loves us because he created us. We as people create life, but yet, we may not even love that life we have created. Not only that, but we may not love the partner who aided in creating a life, we call a baby. This question differs from individual to individual. Personally, I look for Godly character in people. Do they love God? Do they believe in Jesus Christ, the Son of God? Are they nice? Do they love their parents? Do they love people? Do they love children? Do they love the Church? Can they get along with their enemies? We all have enemies whether we admit it or not. It is how we treat them that makes a difference. God gave us a roadmap for loving other people.

"Human beings are very fickle. How do we determine who is loveable? and who is not?"

The best example God gave to us was his Son, Jesus Christ. When we look at Jesus' life, we see so much love and compassion. There is so much forgiveness and suffering. Loving others does cause pain sometimes. The pain is not always intentional, but it happens, nevertheless. We as individuals pick and choose whom we shall love, but God loves us all. For it is written, **"For God so loved the world, that He gave His only begotten Son, that whosoever believeth in Him should not perish, but have everlasting life"** [John 3:16]. This is a powerful statement. God loved the world and gave His unique Son as a demonstration of His love. How many of us could truly give up our child for a world that does not even care about our existence? How can we give our best to someone who could care less? This is exactly what God did! He cared for the unlovable; at least that's what we call some people. So, then I now pose the question to you. Who is loveable in your eyesight? Does your view match that of God? Or does it merely make you comfortable? How can you mold yourself into God's way of loving someone? How can you justify your perception of love? Is there someone you need to love today? Is there someone that needs your love today? Seek and you shall find. Love is only a step away. Find within your heart and mind to love someone near you.

8

Find a way to step out of your prejudices and open your heart to new ideas, new experiences, and new ways of giving. Find the love that is locked away in your heart and spread it around to someone or several people to enhance the rest of your life here on earth. You have the rest of your life to demonstrate the love that God has given to you. Some people will, however, be very easy to love while others will be a challenge. Those that are a challenge will take every ounce of energy to perform the tasks that you know in your heart that God has ordained for you to do. It is through God's Spirit that you will need to depend on for strength, wisdom, and understanding. Strength and understanding will be the most valuable instruments that you will use when trying to reach out to the "unloveable". They are an enormous challenge. It will take prayer, prayer, and much more prayer to accomplish this mission in your life. It can, however, be achieved. The key to success is not giving up. This mission will drain you but know that God is with you, and He will sustain you always. God will place people in your path that will guide you. You may not be able to successfully complete this mission by yourself. Reach out to friends, family, and familiar acquaintances for any needed help. Is there someone you can love today? Can they benefit from what you have to give? Can you benefit from giving love to them? Will your love help them in any way?

Give love, and let God open more opportunities for you to be loved!!!

Chapter 4

I Hurt How Can I Love Someone

Pain comes in many forms. They can be backaches, headaches, broken bones, chronic joint pains, arthritis, sicknesses, diseases, and a broken heart. These pains dictate how we treat others as well as ourselves. Sometimes, it is easier to treat others nicer than ourselves. Why is this? Do we want to hide our true feelings? Do we want others to like us? Do we care more about what others think of us? Do we feel distant from our troubles and worries when we are with others? Do others take our minds off of ourselves? These are all valid questions.

We each have different answers. We each also have different solutions to our problems. I do believe that your problems are different from my problems. That is because you are different from me. We may have the same diagnosis, and the same symptoms, but because of your individuality, your problem is therefore different than mine. I want you to realize that your pain can be expressed freely. I want you to take the time to relay to me how you feel. I may or may not offer an opinion. I just may listen to your ailments. You see, I may not have the answers you need to recover from your pain. I may not have the knowledge to diagnose a remedy for your struggle, but what I do have is a willing heart to listen to your grief and woes. Jesus is the only person I have encountered that knows exactly what pains you have. He cares about your troubles, toils, and tribulations. I on the other hand care about you. I care about what is ailing you, what is stressing you, and what is hurting you. I can not fix the problem or stop it from occurring. The love of Jesus that is in my heart helps me to comfort you in your struggles. The love of Jesus helps me to give what I have to you in your times of need or want. It is through the love of Jesus that I too find comfort and strength.

Jesus is the One that I long for when times get difficult and lonely. Jesus directs me to people who can shoulder my pains during difficult situations such as grief and illness pains. Is there someone you can call on when your pain gets unbearable? Is there someone you can converse with when a troubles arise? Call on Jesus for the company you need when you do not have human companionship. Ask Jesus to send someone to hold your trembling hand until you are strong enough to endure on your own. Through pain, we find it difficult to let someone close to us. **Finding Love in the Midst of Pain** is hard and to love during this time is even harder. During this stage in our lives, we are vulnerable, and we don't want to suffer anymore. Pain is difficult within itself. Why add hurt to injury? Why allow someone to deepen the wound? If we reach out to others during our crises, will we get hurt? There is a strong possibility we will, but we have to do it anyway. We don't just give love in good and happy times, but we give it in our sad, lonely, and desperate times as well. I must say, however, that it is more difficult to love when you are hurting. This is because we don't want our pain enlarged.

> *"Love is not something we can turn on and off like a light switch. Love is embedded in us."*

We don't want our pain to be unbearable. We want our pain to dissolve in someone's love. We want our pain to be absorbed by the people we love the most like a sponge. We want to be loved when we are in pain. This is the time for reciprocating. During our pain is the time we want to feel love and not show love. Pain brings out the worst in us. It is the time in our lives when we cry more, get more frustrated, get angrier, speak harsher, get quieter, withdraw, and some people just downright shut down. Pain causes emotions that are not easily overcome. Where do we find solace for our pain? Where do we find the strength to endure while in the midst of pain? Where do we search for love during this crisis time?

One may say "find a beloved friend or companion". Another may say just "ride it out". Others may say "see a counselor". There are others who may say "read the Bible". Doctors may say "take these pills". All these answers are valid, and all have great potential in working. You are the best person to determine what the right answer is. You know what is best for you. You know what makes you feel better. It may require that you do a combination of things such as read your Bible, take pills, and call a beloved friend or companion. There are no wrong answers and there is no one right answer. **There is, however, an answer!!!**

Finding the answer is always the most difficult part of any situation. The scripture says, "Love never faileth". Find love to aid you through your journey of pain. Love is powerful medicine. The problem may not be love but where to find it. **Finding Love in the Midst of Pain** can be very difficult because sometimes others may not realize how important your need for love at that moment is. They may not understand your desperation. They may not understand how much you are hurting. So, reaching out to someone in the midst of your pain can be made worse by their rejection. Rejection can hurt more than the actual pain, but it is a chance you must take to alleviate the current pain you are feeling. No one wants to be rejected. When you are in pain, the last thing you want is ridicule, embarrassment, or a downright "no". No can come in the form of "I don't have time right now"; "is there someone else you can call"; "you caught me at a bad time"; "I don't have time for this"; "just get over it"; "everyone suffers so what makes you think yours is so different"; and the list goes on and on. The scripture says, "Pain endures for a night, but joy comes in the morning". A night can seem like an eternity when you are in pain. When in pain, all you want is "relief". It doesn't matter how, or what way it comes. You just want relief. Jesus Christ brings relief to our situations. He gives us what others sometimes seem to forget to do. That is. Put us on the priority list. He listens to our cares and woes. He makes us feel as if our pain is the most important thing. He has to save that day. He will gently caress our bodies and makes us know that it shall be all right. He brings comfort and joy. He sustains us. He allows us to bear our troubles and burdens on him freely. He does not turn His face away from us. He opens His arms and heart to us. He gives us a refuge, a place to dwell, a place to shed our tears, a place to cry out (loudly if need be), and He gives us His Holy Word. It is through the scriptures we are able to find words of comfort for our troubled bodies. From the His Holy Word, we are able to find peace for our troubled spirit. From His Holy Word, we are able to **Find Love in the Midst of our Pain**.

The scripture tells us "His grace is sufficient" (2 Corinthians 12:9)! In our spirit, we shout hallelujah, thank you Jesus, and thank you for one more sunny day! Jesus can help us **Find Love in the Midst of our Pain**. When He comes to our rescue, we are excited, joyful, and oh-so glad.

Chapter 5

I'm Not Whole How Can I Love

What is wholeness? How do I obtain it? Does it affect my ability to love or be loved! The Bible speaks of a woman who had an issue with her blood. When she came into contact with Jesus, she touched the hem of His garment. After touching Him, she was made whole. She no longer had the ailment that had plagued her for twelve long years. She was no longer ostracized, she was no longer lonely, and she was no longer sick in her body. Can illness rob you of loving? Does loving come easier with illness? With these questions, we sometime wonder if love can be achieved.

> *"We long to be loved during these times of despair."*

We find ourselves wishing for strength, patience, and the understanding of human compassion. We look deep inside ourselves, and we find that sometimes it is difficult to reach the plateau of perseverance. We look for wisdom to aid us in our quest for knowledge. Loving someone during times we are not whole is difficult. We do not have the desire, passion, compassion, patience, or willingness to produce love in our weakness. When we are not whole or complete, we give incompleteness to those around us. We do, however, long for those we love to still desire us, and give us what we feel we are missing the most. That is love.

When we are not whole, we feel as if something special has departed from us. We feel as if we are drowning in our sorrows and woes. We feel as if tomorrow will bring more pain and misery. We feel as if life is something to be endured and not enjoyed. We search for love, but we can't give it completely. We can only give to others a form of love because that is all we have to give. For some people, a form is all that will be required of you when you are not whole or complete. Others will desire that you give as much as you can gather up. Then, there are those that will desire that you relax and feel their love and comfort. Those who let you relax, understand that you are needy, and they will not demand anything unreasonable or complex from you. They will allow you to lean on them. They will be a pillow to soften your painful areas. They will be your weeping blanket and caress you until the tears stop flowing. They will be the encouragement you need to pursue one more challenging day. They will be love.

Since, they are love, you will not have to be love. All you will have to do is embrace their compassion, their stalwart arms, their loving eyes, and their warming passion. It is in times when you are not whole that the ones you loved during the wholeness years will come and rejuvenate you. That is what you need the most. Time to rejuvenate, time to heal, time to feel, and time to exist. This is what you need. It is during this mode of operation that you find strength, courage, wisdom, and a sense of ease that you begin to develop your wholeness. When you are not whole, you feel drained and incomplete. The love you have inside is locked away deep down in the tresses of despair. All you need and desire is for someone, anyone to flood your heart with their love to unlock the love that is hidden deep in your heart. You need someone to unleash the passion, zeal, and gallantry of noble compassion. You need to feel complete. You need to feel desired. You need to feel loved! The touch of a warm body would bring so much joy. The whisper of a gentle voice filled with tenderness would be oh-so welcomed. The invitation of outstretched arms would be ever so inviting. You need a place to collapse without being criticized. So, when you are not whole, you can not love. You need to feel love when wholeness escapes you. You need to feel love when wholeness forsakes you. You need to feel love when wholeness misplaces you. Who can make you whole again? Jesus Christ of Nazareth will! Why would you want to be whole anyway? It is really very simple. The answer is "to love again". There is nothing on earth better than love. There is nothing on earth better than being loved. Love generates passion, zest, compassion, zeal, strength, mobility, joy, happiness, and all the emotions that the human brain can interpret. Humans are special creatures. They were designed with such perfection that one must stand in awe of the creature, God. God in His infinite wisdom placed some incredible senses into mankind. When everything is functioning properly, the human body is such a fantastic work of art. When something is out of order, it can cause such chaos that it can make the most loveable person very undesirable. This is why we as humans want to be whole. We want to be desirable. We want to love and be loved.

What good is life without loving someone special? What good is life when there is no one to love us in return? We want to feel needed. We want to feel complete. We want to be whole. There are times, however when wholeness will be impossible. This can be due to an illness, sickness, loss of a limb, loss of vision, or just lost in the sinfulness of the world. When these circumstances occur, we need someone to stand in the gap for us. We need someone to build a bridge of unity in our stead. We need someone to pull us to the next plateau of life. There is that word, life. Life can be full of ups and downs. Life can cause heartaches and pains, but it is all that we have been given. That is why it is so important to find someone to love and someone to love you back. Love makes life worth living. Jesus said in John 14:6, "I am the way, the truth, and the life: no man cometh unto the Father, but by me". Jesus brings life to our world. Jesus brings meaning to our existence. Jesus brings us wholeness when others find us incomplete. Jesus brings us what we need the most. That is love! We may not all get the opportunity to touch Him like the woman with the issue of blood. We may not all get the opportunity to hear Him say, "Thou art whole". We do, however, get the opportunity to spend life eternally with Him once we decide we want Him in our life. Wholeness, can I have it? Wholeness, should I desire it? Wholeness, can I obtain it? The answer to each question is yes. It can be found, obtained, and given through love. Search the scriptures in your bible, search your friend, and search your family to obtain the love you need to be made whole.

Once you find it, please don't let it go! Hold on to love for dear life because it is your life. Your life is important and worth fighting for. Your life is worth more than silver and more precious than gold.

Your life is desirable to all those who care and love you. You must come to the conscious decision to find love within yourself. You must find peace with your life as it is now until things get better. Love is the doorway to finding wholeness and completeness. I charge you to open your heart to someone who is willing to love you. I charge you to let yourself be loved. I charge you to surrender your heart to someone special. Then, you will understand how important it is to be loved, and how important it is to love. **Truly, there is nothing better than love, than love itself!!!**

Chapter 6

I Want To Love

Love is such a small word, but it has such a tremendous meaning. When I think of the word love, I think of my family, especially my children. From the time that I learned that I had conceived, I loved them. Before they were born into this world, here on earth, I loved them. Love has no limits nor does it have boundaries. I remember how great it was to see their little faces, hands, and feet the day of their birth. I checked them thoroughly, just as the doctors had done with their medical instrument. I only had visual tools to test their wellness.

After many disappointments through the years, I forgot how to love, but I wanted to be love by someone special. My body was not the same mentally nor physically, but I wanted to be whole and loved. Wholeness was not an option for me anymore. I had been diagnosed with an incurable disease. How can I expect to be loved? Who would desire me in the present state that I had become. I remember the Bible verse in John 14:1, "Let not your heart be troubled, you believe in God, believe also in me". I was troubled, but I did believe in Jesus Christ. I spent times trying to heal myself, but each time I failed. Each time a little of me died. Each time I was becoming someone that I didn't know or want to become. How was I going to be loved? I searched the Bible and prayed daily looking for answers. Then, it dawned on me. Test the waters and be one about your illness and see if someone can find you loveable. I had found the inner strength that I needed to search for someone to love me I wanted to be loved. Had I found peace, had I found acceptance, had I given up on healing, what had I done that made me desire love? The answer to that question rang out in my mind. You found the desire and the want from reading "Song of Solomon" from the Bible.

> *"I didn't love myself because I was no longer the person that I had grown to love. If I could not love myself as I was now, who could pull up the slack and love me as I am with this new life that I would have to lead."*

How had this happened? Why was I gravitating to this book of the Bible? Why was I wanting what the romantics in this story had? Why did I find a love story to fill my nights and free daytime? Why was I wanting to have stalwart arms to hold me close and tell me that "you are not alone"? Most of the time I felt alone. I really didn't have anyone who understood what I was going through. My doctor wasn't any help. She could only prescribe medication because she had not personally dealt with the day-to-day issues I had. Others that came to her office with similar or the same diagnosis didn't have the same experience I had. So again, why did I want to be loved? The songwriter put it best by saying "there's nothing better than love what in the world are you waiting for". I guess I must have been listening to the lyrics. I was ready! Can I find someone, especially a handsome man, who could love me despite my illness? Could he accept me as I had become? Could he find love in his heart for me? I needed to know if this was possible. I was willing to test the waters to find out. Could I be honest and still be loved? Could I be diseased and still be desired? Could I be willing to love and be loved back? So many questions, but who held the answers? Finally, could I love myself more than he loved me? Jesus could. What about a mortal man? I was ready to find out! Was I ready to adventure into the realm of loving another human? Was I ready to be rejected or accepted? Was I ready to love?

Chapter 7

I Found Him

The Bible says seek and ye shall find. I had a quest. It was to find a mortal man that could love me knowing that I was not a whole and healthy person. I believe that I presented a pretty physical appearance and an accompanying attitude. I had begun to feel better about myself with the help of modern medicine. I still had bad days, but I also had good days. The good days were pleasant and easy to carry out day-to-day tasks such as cooking, working a full-time job, cleaning, and rearing my two children. On bad days, it was a struggle to do anything, but with a little help from others and long talks with my mother, I managed to handle things that came my way.

As I began to become stronger in my physical body, my spiritual body was at a heightened state. I loved God more and more. Jesus was truly a friend indeed. He plagued my dreams and my thoughts. I went to sleep with Him on my mind, and He was the first thing I thought of in the morning light. Jesus had given me the hope and peace that I needed to enjoy the hustle and bustle of everyday life. He was my way maker, my company keeper, my dew in the morning, and my heavenly Savior. My nights with Him were so wonderful. He brought joy and excitement to my life. If I was troubled, He could calm me. If I had questions, He could answer me. He gave me what I could not get from my husband. My husband did not and would not take the time to learn about what was ailing me, nor did he want to discuss how I felt or my feelings. He just wanted to ignore the diagnosis and pretend that everything was ok, but things were not ok.

I needed someone who would listen to my grieves and woes. I needed someone who was strong and could bare my pain. I need a man that could handle storms and still be manly. I needed a person who would not be frightened of what I had to say. I wanted someone whom I could contact at any time, and who would be available to me. How many people could fit this bill? How many people would be willing to help me, or even consider helping me? I had reached out to some, but they felt like my husband, or they would take over the conversation and describe their pains and woes. Could I find someone who could focus on me? All my life, I had put others before me, but now I needed someone to put me first. I want to be the center of someone's attention. Could such a person exist? Yes, he did! I found that man that I needed. He desired to help me through my difficult times. He was strong and quiet. He was kind to me and others. Sometimes, I had the ability to try his patience. When I did, he would take a deep breath and continue to listen. He was my sounding board. He was my go-to person. We developed a friendship like none I have ever had. During my difficult days, he would listen to me talk, and not interrupt or voice his opinion. He was a listener. Sometimes, that was not what I wanted, but that is what he gave. As time rolled on, he desired to be my big brother.

That was a great comfort to me because I had always wanted a big brother that could step in and stand up for me. He was willing to do that. He was able to do that. He did that. Finding him was a blessing from God. He was able to love me when I thought maybe no one would. He befriended me as I had desired. He made time for me. I could even call him in the early mornings or in the late evenings or during lunch hour. He made himself available. I guess that was what I truly needed. I needed someone to be there for me. I needed someone to lean on. I needed someone to be sympathetic to my needs. I found that with him. I think the most outstanding thing about him was that he looked like Jesus. Sometimes, I could not tell them apart. My dreams and my reality were somehow merging. At times, I felt as if Jesus was using his body to talk to me. I would ask him questions about some advice he gave, and he would not remember saying anything. It was sometimes confusing because I would come back and thank him for what he had said in some of our conversations, and he would not have a clue. The spirit of God can fall on anyone. I felt that Jesus was communicating with me through him. The advice that was given to me gave me strength, compassion, understanding, and joy. The advice would always fit the circumstances. Jesus can provide and guide us from heaven through other people. I have personally been told several times that I had been "an answer to a prayer". Jesus used an earthly vessel to bring to me the love that I desired and wanted. That is the most special thing about Jesus Christ and His Father. They will give you the desires of your heart. God has never failed me. I can and will always count on Him no matter what state I am in. There will come a day when He will be all I need, and other days He will send someone who has the strength and willingness to hold me up. I thank God for sending me a big brother who is now a great friend. I needed a big brother and now I just need him as a friend. God knows what we need when we need it. I am truly thankful for the new friends I have found to help me on my present journey. I know God had a hand in the association. Our friendship grows as the years go by. Life has ups and life has downs. I am grateful to God for allowing me to find someone who was willing to share my struggles. Life is meant to be shared. God never intended us to be on this journey by ourselves. Even the scriptures tell us that "it is not good for man to be alone". He is out there. Keep searching until you find him!

Truly, I Found Love In The Midst Of Pain!!!!!

www.ingramcontent.com/pod-product-compliance
Lightning Source LLC
LaVergne TN
LVHW021739060526
838200LV00052B/3356